A 1960s Edinb

Birth: 'the coming into

In the bleak mid-winter, Dickens' Christmas stories give the reader images of hope and light; warmth and joy; as well as transformation and resurrection. However, the light is tempered by the darkness and cold too which makes it even more life enhancing.

The hope comes from spring, surely following winter and the renewal of life as Scrooge is restored to the good values of his boyhood and youth.

Six decades ago in the deep mid-winter of 1958, the Hanlon family moved into the newly built Edinburgh Corporation flats at 6 Oxgangs Avenue to take up residence at 'The Stair'; Charlie and Hilda were full of hope at the beginning of the exciting adventure ahead and novelty of bringing up their family in a new home.

Like the other young families at 'The Stair' they had their dreams and aspirations of the good life and raising their children as well as they could, with all the fun, joys and worries inherent.

At this time, only Michael, the eldest brother had been born; he would only have been around one year old; Brian, Colin and Alan would come along in the following years.

When the family took up their tenancy at 6/7, like the other seven families in residence at 'The Stair', they were issued with a rent book. It records their rent as being eighteen shillings a week.

Most remarkably, Hilda, the last remaining original member at 'The Stair', still has the family's first rent book. It records their date of entry as 15th December, 1958.

In a way the document records the birth of 'The Stair', when one of the original inhabitants first took up residence there and is perhaps a unique document of its type.

Brian speaks humorously about the family's first experience. Hilda recalled the Hoffmann family had already moved in downstairs to 6/2 slightly earlier. The coal-man was delivering coal to our family-Ken and Anne Hoffmann, the author (Peter aged two) and my brother, Iain (aged only a month).

Hilda wanted to buy some coal in too, to heat their new home. However, the coal merchant turned down her request as she lived on the top floor and he mustn't have fancied walking up another three flights of stairs. Given it was mid-winter and Michael, the eldest brother was still only a baby, the stone-hearted coal-man clearly wasn't full of the Christmas spirit.

... *tried to warm himself at the candle*

He reminds me of Ebenezer Scrooge to Bob Cratchit, that '...there will be no coal burned in this office today...'

Hilda must have found a way forward, not only to heat their new top flat home with its fantastic views to the hills and the sea, as well as the prominent Edinburgh Castle, as she and Charlie went on to successfully raise their four boys in a happy household, throughout the decades of the 1960s and 1970s.

'Edinburgh in Snow' William Crozier

Spring and indeed summer followed winter.

In the years and decade of the 1960s that followed, at this time of the seasonal year, my sister Anne, brother Iain and I, whatever our circumstances found that come Christmas, 'Santa Claus' always did us proud. Christmas was always the best and most exciting time of the year for us.

When I say Santa (aka Mother-sometimes with support from Father) did us proud, I don't mean that we were

spoiled or received any expensive presents-indeed, quite
the contrary. And instead, we each received a stocking
which was filled chockfull of imaginative small presents
which were an absolute delight to wake up to on
Christmas morning.

Like most children it was the one evening in the year
when we were keen to go to bed early of our own
accord. And of course, it was the one winter's morning in
the year that we were keen to get up early too!

I'm not too sure how Christmas worked in all the other
households in 'The Stair'. But, perhaps only Norman
Stewart at 6/3 did better than any of the other children, in
terms of expensive presents,

Where we did get a small insight into how the season was
celebrated within other homes was on our return to
school in January.

The teacher always asked each of us individually to tell the
rest of the class about our main present.

Well, we hadn't really received such a thing from Santa-
instead it was just small, charming little serendipities.

I therefore didn't enjoy this and I can recall telling a fib
saying that I had been given a graphic designer's set. Of
course I didn't have a *scooby* what that was, but I was
determined not to be out-gunned by Norman; being an
immediate neighbour and friend, he of course was the

one pupil in the class who knew perfectly well that I had not received any such thing!

Colinton Mains Parish Church

In my mind's eye, Christmas Eve was a very quiet evening in 'The Stair'.

I can recall Father going out on several Christmas Eves to attend the local Watchnight church service, presumably at Colinton Mains Parish Church, the same church which the Swansons at 6/2 attended.

Although we could hear the church bell ring out at St John's Church up the hill, I don't think Father went to the remarkable Reverend Jack Orr's service.

St John's Church bell

Over the years our mother and Mrs Molly Swanson had a reciprocal arrangement whereby Mother gave Gavin and Heather Swanson a wee tin of Woolworths' toffees each whilst we all received something from Molly.

On one memorable Christmas, I received a 'book' from her, but when I opened it, rather than pages, much to my delight, it instead held seven tubes of sweets arranged horizontally inside.

The three Hogg girls up above at 6/3, always received 'girly pressies' and I can recall my sister Anne spending time with Christina, Maureen and Eileen at this time of the year.

I'm much vaguer on how the Blades at 6/6 spent Christmas, other than when Alison, Ruth and Esther Blades could be seen out playing, bouncing around on their new 'Spacehoppers' which were introduced to the United Kingdom in 1969.

Before Anne was born, our grandfather gave Iain and me a bobble Santa each which were full of wrapped toffees. The Santa figure is delightful and has been carefully looked after these past fifty years; and each year we bring the two Santas down from the attic to be displayed. The Swansons received a similar Santa figure too, but they had less jolly faces.

The Hanlons and the Blades often hung linked paper ring decorations in their living rooms which reached from corner to corner across the ceiling.

I used to regret that we were more conservative with only our individual Woolworths' decorations on display.

Today, I appreciate how attractive and aesthetically pleasing they are. However, there wasn't the same crowded and crude effect, which as a young boy I naturally liked and preferred.

I suspect Woolworths did Mother and many other parents proud over the decades.

On going to bed on Christmas Eve each of the three of us would leave one of our mother's nylon stockings at the foot of our beds.

In the early morning I was always the first of us to awake. I would crawl down to the foot of the bed and reach out to see if Santa had arrived-YES!-oh the excitement of feeling the bulkiness of the misshapen stocking full of surprises-it was the most wonderful sensation in the world!

'It's Christmas!', I would bellow out, 'It's Christmas!' I would shout, as I jumped down from the top bunk bed to the floor to switch on the bedroom light and awaken the others.

The stockings were quite wonderful and filled with torches; little games; Yogi Bear or Huckleberry Hound picture books; perhaps a young person's novel; colouring books and pens; a selection box; some gold coins; an orange and an apple and a half crown; and the obligatory 'Broons' or 'Oor Wullie' annual in later years.

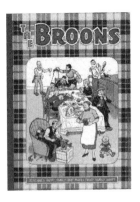

Anne meanwhile would get some 'girly stuff'. I particularly recall a delightful peach smelling cream; whilst Iain might receive a toy car, perhaps a 'Corgi' or some 'Matchbox' cars.

On one occasion when quite young I got a leather football and football boots-the first boy in the immediate neighbourhood to receive such sports items; however it was the old fashioned heavy leather ball and big unwieldy boots which would have taken a 'Messi' to able to control the ball with.

In our innocence we would then rush through to awaken our parents to show them what 'Santa' had brought us!

These Christmas mornings were simple little affairs, but wonderful; no matter how poor we might be, Mother ensured that these were magical occasions every year for us, from being very small children right through and into our teens; happy times and very, very sweet memories, which I've never forgotten.

Christmas Day itself was rather like Sundays, only quieter. We saw very little of what went on in the rest of 'The Stair' because our grandfather would collect us all mid-morning in his large Ford Zephyr car with its leather bench seats and drive us all down to Portobello for the day, not returning us home to Oxgangs until late in the evening.

We always spent the whole day at our grandparents' home at Durham Road, Portobello. I therefore have no intimate knowledge of how the Swansons; the Stewarts; the Hoggs; the Smiths; the Blades; the Hanlons; or the Duffys spent their Christmas Day.

However, Christmas Day is the most popular church day of the year, so I could surmise that the Swansons probably attended Colinton Mains Parish Church of Scotland; meanwhile, the Blades will have gone along to one of the Baptist churches; whilst the Duffys will have celebrated Christ's birth at St Marks Roman Catholic Church, Oxgangs Avenue.

St Mark's RC Church

The drive from Oxgangs down to Portobello from 'The Stair' was always the quietest of the whole year. Sundays were normally quiet, but on Christmas Day there were even fewer cars on the road and we just sailed down as if we were the Royal Family.

Reverend Walker Skating Duddingston Loch, Henry Raeburn

We drove through Greenbank, Morningside and along Grange Road and on through the Queen's Park passing Duddingston Loch on the right, always looking out for the skating minister as we assumed it was his home!

On the bad bend outside the 12th century Duddingston Kirk our grandfather always blared the car's horn loudly, impishly hoping it was midway through the chaplain's sermon.

We then wended our way down to Nana's and the excitement of turning on to the foot of Durham Road with its fine small Edwardian mansion-houses.

12th century, Dudingston Kirk

It was our grandmother who made Christmas the day that it was.

She would be there to greet us in the hallway and we would give her a formal light kiss on the cheek.

Although she loved us all very dearly, she wasn't effusive and instead had more of the demeanour of a conservative English gentlewoman's restraint.

Instead she expressed her great love for family and to many others through innumerable acts of kindness over the years and the decades.

The hall looked resplendent; there would be a flower arrangement on a dark antique table and for once the royal blue carpet had been hoovered clean.

As a busy artist, jeweller, pottery decorator, lace-woman and gardener our grandmother didn't want to be remembered for dusting the house-she had far more important priorities, but Christmas was an exception.

And, because her house resembled the 'Old Curiosity Shop', full of fascinating antiques and interesting items from throughout the world, the hall really didn't need any Christmas décor. Although, I suppose one could have hung some tinsel from the African buffalo's antlers high on one wall!

In later years I lived there from the winter of 1972 and whenever I invited a friend, a colleague or a journalist into her front room, their first comment on entering was always 'What a fascinating room this is!'

Apart from the tiny kitchen, her house was perfect to host the large Christmas gatherings which took place there for over half a century.

The hatch linking the kitchen to the sitting room was a clever little idea. As the kitchen had no work space or work tops at all, the Buchan's pottery casseroles containing hot vegetables were placed there and also delicately balanced on top of the old washing machine.

Grandma Jo had the most wonderful grace under pressure-I never saw her get flustered. Indeed, when I think about it I never recall her raising her voice in all the subsequent years that I stayed with her. The only hint of any colourful language emanating from the kitchen would be from Father working hard as he whipped the cream by hand.

Our grandmother served up those wonderful Christmas dinners through the magic little hatch, year in and year out, until she was well into her eighties, when I took over hosting Christmas as the 'Laird 'O Plewlands'; then at West Mill, Colinton; and for a few years at Moorlands, Dingwall.

The first course was usually home-made soup. This was followed by the traditional roast turkey; mashed and roasted potatoes; various vegetables; and two types of stuffing-sage and onion and sausage-meat, with gravy. And. despite being a butcher, our grandfather never carved the bird and instead that too was also left to our grandmother-she was very much the matriarch.

The dining table was lovely to behold. With the eye of the trained artist the table was laid out with colourful antiques and glassware. It looked like something out of a Dickens novel. There would also be beer, lemonade and as we children got older, the excitement of having some 'Woodpeckers Cider' too.

'Christmas Dinner', Peter Hoffmann

Around the table the craic was good-some teasing-some wit-some awful jokes-pulling crackers and several of us cajoling our grandmother to 'Come on through Josephine and enjoy your dinner too!'

Atypically, she was always the last to take a seat at the table and join the extended family.

There were various puddings-trifles, a mix of milk and water jellies and single, double and whipped cream. However, before we could face our pudding we children would often go outside into the winter air and stroll around the back garden to help regain our appetites.

'The Wonderful Pudding' Sol Eytinge, Jr.

Grandma Jo always prepared a home-made Christmas plum pudding and we children would 'ooh and ahh' when the brandy was poured on top of it and lit. The flame puffed up almost taking our eyebrows off.

To accompany the pudding there was both custard and ice cream, the latter coming from either the wonderful Arcari's, Portobello or Lucas, Musselburgh, Italian ice cream shops which served Edinburgh residents so well over the years.

Because of the large number of people around the old dining table-the very young; the young; adults; the middle aged; the old; and the very old, these occasions were quite magical throughout the decade of the 1960s. The age range of those sitting around the table covered approximately ninety years, thus stretching back to when Queen Victoria was on the throne.

Sometimes there would be a dozen or so of us present.

Was it Old Aunt Mary or our great-grandmother, Wee Nana, who always said 'Now, Josephine...where's the silver spoon...you know I can't *possibly* eat my pudding without it!'

And, when I was very young, her husband, 'The Miser' aka Pumpa (our great-grandfather) tried to slip me a penny, which I turned down-much to his amusement!

Once Christmas Dinner was over and before the Queen came on the television to broadcast to the nation, the adults would retire gratefully to various rooms throughout the house to allow their food to digest.

Mother would enjoy a snooze in one of the bedrooms, usually my grandmother's south facing room, which always had a very comforting and quiet feel to it. Meanwhile, Aunt Heather would be in the kitchen with her sleeves rolled up, washing dishes in the sink, often with Father giving her a helping hand.

Others would find a spot on a spare sofa, put their feet up and place their head on a soft cushion and shortly be happily asleep.

We children might go out to the garden for a while.

It was good to go out with Iain from the warmth of the house and in to the fresh cold air in the winter garden. We enjoyed having a blether about our presents or kicking a ball around.

In its bare winter December state the garden had a completely different feel to July when it was lush and adorned in its summer clothes. In its hibernated state all that remained were the skeletons and structures of trees, hedges and shrubs.

And as the afternoon coolness descended and the light began to disappear, I enjoyed the quiet and solitude of the garden and the slightly brooding presence of the season.

All that separated the light from the dark, the cold from the warmth, was a solitary door.

It made me think of some lines from Buchan's 'The Power-House' where the hero, Sir Edward Leithen is told: 'You think that a wall as solid as the earth separates civilisation from barbarism. I tell you the division is a thread, a sheet of glass. A touch here, a push there, and you bring back the reign of Saturn.'

And then, it was braw to go back into the warmth of the house and the bosom of the family and to be reminded once again, that it was still Christmas Day!

After the Queen's broadcast a highlight for me was to sit quietly in the 'Smoking Room' at the front of the house. This was the front room, which was a fascinating room to be in, because it was full of antiques, paintings, glassware, snuff bottles and old French clocks.

I sat on the big old sofa alongside my grandfather, whilst my great grandfather and father sat on the large squishy chairs opposite.

There was a large old gramophone come radio cabinet in the corner and a Christmas tree in the bay window.

It was here that the men retired to enjoy the home-made sweets which our grandmother made annually for Christmas-marzipan and walnuts; peppermint creams; fudge et al.

But most of all I liked when the men enjoyed a cigar. I loved the smell of the cigar smoke. It's a smell which immediately transports me back through the mists of time.

I loved sitting quietly, listening to my great-grandfather, grandfather and father talking and conversing. I always kept very quiet and tried not to be intrusive in case I wasn't allowed to stay.

And, as the light began to slowly fade and darkness fell and the street-lights flickered on outside, we switched the Christmas tree lights on. The lights were a novelty as we didn't have them back at 'The Stair' at 6/2 Oxgangs Avenue.

In that room, surrounded by three older generations, I felt part of a line going back to Victorian times.

I also felt warm, secure and at peace. I didn't want these moments to end and savoured the hour or two before someone would look around the door to say that 'Tea was now being served up and would the men come through and join the rest of the party.'

We would all troop through to enjoy some fresh cut bread, salad and some 'John West' salmon which was a luxury item back in the 1960s. There would also be a variety of shortbread, Christmas cake, mincemeat pies and for the gutsy perhaps seconds of trifle and cream.

By then a good fire was blazing in the grate and one of the nice things about Christmas Day compared to our Sunday visitations was that we got to stay on a little longer into the evening.

Our grandfather would give our great-grandparents a lift back home to London Road, Dalkeith, before then returning the seven or so miles back to Portobello to give the Hoffmanns a lift back home to Oxgangs Avenue and 'The Stair'.

On the way home to Oxgangs in the car, we would all snuggle up together to keep warm. However, unlike the journey down which was taken in the eager anticipation of a family Christmas Day moving towards its zenith in the bright winter sunshine, come the end of this most special of days, it was now appropriately dark, as Christmas began to die its death.

Now passing Duddingston Loch on our left, it was so black out, that we couldn't really see the loch unless the moon was out and reflected upon its surface, dancing on the dark waters.

Duddingston Loch by Moonlight, Charles Lees

And this in contrast to a century before, when Robert Louis Stevenson enjoyed the season and wrote in the winter of 1874 of looking down upon the skaters on the frozen loch flitting around under the light from the moon and the lit torches.

Leaving the Queens Park, we children played a game to see who could count the most lit Christmas trees in sitting room windows along Grange Road, Morningside and Greenbank, before we descended into Oxgangs.

And then, of a sudden, we were back from where we'd started out.

It was of course a stark contrast coming home to 6/2. The house was quiet. It was cold. And the one bar electric fire would be immediately switched on.

However, it was slightly more inviting than usual, because the Christmas tree decorated the corner of the living room and we had the pleasure of coming back home to our presents.

Before going to bed I would carefully re-pack my stocking with my presents and place it at the end of my bed to try to recreate the Christmas morning experience when I awoke on Boxing Day.

However, it was never the same.

Printed in Poland
by Amazon Fulfillment
Poland Sp. z o.o., Wrocław